10 PSAT Vocabulary Practice Tests

Paul G Simpson IV

with the Staff of Test Professors™

Library of Congress Control Number: 2011914069

ISBN: 978-1-937599-00-3

Acknowledgements

Special thanks to David Hao for yet another instance of hard work and dedication. Finally, thanks to all of our students, past and present, without whom this book would not have been possible.

10 PSAT VOCABULARY PRACTICE TESTS

PSAT VOCABULARY PRACTICE TEST 1

Suggested Time: 5 minutes
8 Questions

Directions: In context, choose the word(s) that fits the sentence best.

1. The ----- of the shipwreck survivors was later dismissed, when it was ----- that they were not rescued from the ocean but from a bathtub.

   (A) reinforcement…rebutted
   (B) contradiction…clarified
   (C) account…confirmed
   (D) substantiation…stressed
   (E) depiction…disproved

2. Angela ----- the severity of her problems by ----- them in great detail, beginning with her birth.

   (A) corroborated…refuting
   (B) debunked…highlighting
   (C) reinforced…elucidating
   (D) challenged…substantiating
   (E) confirmed…invalidating

3. Mencken gained a deserved reputation as a ----- who questioned everything and took nothing at face value.

   (A) pessimist   (B) miser   (C) hedonist
       (D) spendthrift   (E) skeptic

4. Joanne's justification for her answer was so strong that her adversary had trouble countering it and was left gaping in silent -----.

   (A) elucidation   (B) perplexity   (C) assertion
       (D) punctuation   (E) confirmation

5. Mrs. Affluence is widely known as a -----, who has given millions of dollars to charity and whose altruism has helped countless penurious people.

   (A) miser   (B) pauper   (C) glutton
       (D) conformist   (E) philanthropist

6. Though the couple's relationship had appeared to be filled only with -----, their later separation hinted at the couple's growing ----- and apathy.

   (A) spite…obsequiousness
   (B) nonchalance…calumny
   (C) élan…disinterest
   (D) castigation…approbation
   (E) enmity…rebuff

7. The bookstore's customers comprised ----- group, one of heterogeneous backgrounds and disparate tastes.

   (A) a ravenous   (B) a digressive   (C) a motley
       (D) a prodigal   (E) an incognito

8. Though skeptics doubt his claim's -----, he still maintains that he played only a tangential, ----- role in the Sandwich Riots of 1929.

   (A) temerity…trenchant
   (B) excoriation…disparate
   (C) veracity…incidental
   (D) inscrutability…touted
   (E) spuriousness…élan

Suggested Time: 3 minutes
5 Questions

> **Directions:** In context, choose the word(s) that fits the sentence best.

1. The teacher's union rejected the school's -----, leaving the dispute without a -----.

   (A) derision…prevalence
   (B) document…discrepancy
   (C) accolades…disclosure
   (D) empathy…prevalence
   (E) proposal…resolution

2. Standardized test makers are ----- by nature, often living alone in dark, subterranean caves.

   (A) reclusive (B) superfluous (C) precocious
   (D) verbose (E) meticulous

3. Straka stunned his neighbors by shedding his normal hesitancy and ----- choosing to mow his front lawn.

   (A) irresolutely (B) cogently (C) unequivocally
   (D) lastingly (E) submissively

4. The politician's critics accused him of ----- on the issue of war, claiming he was unable to take a decisive stand.

   (A) assenting (B) avoiding (C) attributing
   (D) dissenting (E) equivocating

5. Her ----- and wariness in new social settings should not be construed as hostility because she, in fact, was ----- person who loved nothing more than to chat and laugh with others.

   (A) diffidence…an amicable
   (B) fecklessness…an ambivalent
   (C) triteness…a vacillating
   (D) impediment…a hapless
   (E) mollification…a prosaic

Suggested Time: 4 minutes
6 Questions

Directions: In context, choose the word(s) that fits the sentence best.

1. Mrs. Dillard was no mere ----- in the area of antique pickles; indeed, she was renowned as an expert.

   (A) sage   (B) eccentric   (C) dilettante
      (D) pacifist   (E) advocate

2. Reading over the question, she soon realized that most of its words were -----; she didn't need them to find the correct answer.

   (A) precocious   (B) languid   (C) extraneous
      (D) succinct   (E) concurring

3. The test day was a ----- event; the students marked it with solemnity and a tinge of sadness.

   (A) hackneyed   (B) scanty   (C) somber
      (D) benevolent   (E) superfluous

4. Professor Fuentes remained ----- about the convicted inmate's guilt and worked to ----- her on the basis of DNA evidence.

   (A) astute…acclaim
   (B) impregnable…vindicate
   (C) indolent…preclude
   (D) despondent…avoid
   (E) dubious…exonerate

5. In contrast to her sister's ----- reaction to the crowd, Jen greeted it with ----- and enthusiasm.

   (A) anomalous…acrimony
   (B) marred...erroneousness
   (C) flagrant…renunciation
   (D) morose…ebullience
   (E) eloquent…euphemism

6. Her ----- research, accomplished over long decades, finally paid off with her discovery of the location of Napoleon's toothbrush.

   (A) specious   (B) assiduous   (C) affable
      (D) malicious   (E) gregarious

Practice Test 1
Answer Key and Explanations

Section 1

1. (C) account...confirmed
2. (C) reinforced...elucidating
3. (E) skeptic
4. (B) perplexity
5. (E) philanthropist
6. (C) élan...disinterest
7. (C) a motley
8. (C) veracity...incidental

Section 2

1. (E) proposal...resolution
2. (A) reclusive
3. (C) unequivocally
4. (E) equivocating
5. (A) diffidence...an amicable

Section 3

1. (C) dilettante
2. (C) extraneous
3. (C) somber
4. (E) dubious...exonerate
5. (D) morose...ebullience
6. (B) assiduous

Finding Your Percentile Rank

Raw score: Total Number Right – [Total Number Wrong ÷ 4] = _____

Raw Score	Percentile Rank
19	99
18	97
17	93
16	89
15	85
14	80
13	75
12	70
11	65
10	60
9	50
8	45
7	40
6	35
5	30
4	25
3	20
2	15
1	10
0	5
-1 or below	1 - 4

Identifying Strengths and Areas for Improvement

Go back to the test and circle the questions that you answered incorrectly. This review will allow you to see what vocabulary to study more closely. It will also allow you to see what word lists you need to review more carefully. You can also reference *Score-Raising Vocabulary Builder for ACT and SAT Prep*, a companion study guide and vocabulary workbook.

	Section 1	Section 2	Section 3
To Explain	1, 2		
To Argue For	1		
To Emphasize	2		
Confused	4		
Depressed			3, 5
Questioning / Doubtful	3		4
Indifferent / Lazy	6		
Amateur			1
Shy		2, 5	
To Solve		1	
Offer		1	
Irrelevant	8		2
Different / Odd	7		
True / Honest	8		
Passionate	6		
Generous	5		
Sure		3	
Unsure		4	
Free from Blame			4
Cheerful			5
Hard-Working			6
Friendly		5	

Section 1

1. C (account...confirmed:
   to explain...to argue for)

(A) reinforcement...rebutted:
   emphasize... argue against
(B) contradiction...clarified:
   to argue against...to explain
(D) substantiation...stressed:
   to argue for...to emphasize
(E) depiction...disproved:
   to explain ...to argue against

2. C (reinforced...elucidating:
   argue against...explain)

(A) corroborated...refuting:
   to argue for...to argue against
(B) debunked...highlighting:
   argue against...emphasize
(D) challenged...substantiating:
   argue against...argue for
(E) confirmed...invalidating:
   to argue for...to argue against

3. E (skeptic: *questioning*)

(A) pessimist: *unhopeful*
(B) miser: *greedy*
(C) hedonist: *seek pleasure*
(D) spendthrift: *using a lot*

4. B (perplexity: *confused*)

(A) elucidation: *to explain*
(C) assertion: to *argue for*
(D) punctuation: *to emphasize*
(E) confirmation: *to argue for*

5. E (philanthropist: *generous*)

(A) miser: *greedy*
(B) pauper: *poor*
(C) glutton: *greedy*
(D) conformist: *same*

6. C (élan...disinterest:
   passionate...indifferent)

(A) spite...obsequiousness:
   hate...to flatter
(B) nonchalance...calumny:
   indifferent...to insult
(D) castigation...approbation:
   to scold...to praise
(E) enmity...adulation:
   to hate...to flatter

7. C (a motley: *different*)

(A) a ravenous: *greedy*
(B) a digressive: *irrelevant*
(D) a prodigal: *rich*
(E) an incognito: *secretive*

8. C (veracity...incidental:
   honest...irrelevant)

(A) temerity...trenchant:
   brave...relevant
(B) excoriation...disparate:
   to criticize...different
(D) inscrutability...touted:
   secretive...to praise
(E) spuriousness...élan:
   false...passionate

Section 2

1. E (proposal…resolution:
   ***offer…to solve*)**

(A) derision…prevalence:
   insult…widespread
(B) document…discrepancy:
   record…different
(C) accolades…disclosure:
   praise…give
(D) empathy…prevalence:
   feeling…widespread

2. A (reclusive: *shy*)

(B) superfluous: *unnecessary*
(C) precocious: *mature*
(D) verbose: *talkative*
(E) meticulous: *careful*

3. C (unequivocally: *sure*)

(A) irresolutely: *unsure*
(B) cogently: *relevant*
(D) lastingly: *long-lived*
(E) submissively: *obedient*

4. E (equivocating: *unsure*)

(A) assenting: *argue for*
(B) avoiding: *elude*
(C) attributing: *give*
(D) dissenting: *argue against*

5. D (diffidence…an amicable:
   ***shy…friendly*)**

(A) fecklessness…an ambivalent:
   unskilled…unsure
(B) triteness…a vacillating:
   clichéd…unsure
(C) impediment…a hapless:
   stop…unlucky
(E) mollification…motley:
   indifferent…a prosaic

Section 3

1. C (dilettante: *amateur*)

(A) sage: *smart*
(B) eccentric: *different / odd*
(D) pacifist: *believer in peace*
(E) advocate: *argue for*

2. C (extraneous: *irrelevant*)

(A) precocious: *mature*
(B) languid: *lazy / indifferent*
(D) succinct: *short*
(E) concurring: *agree*

3. C (somber: *depressed*)

(A) hackneyed: *clichéd*
(B) scanty: *a little*
(D) benevolent: *generous*
(E) superfluous: *unnecessary*

4. E (dubious…exonerate:
questioning…free from blame)

(A) astute…acclaim:
smart…praise
(B) impregnable…vindicate:
strong…argue for
(C) indolent…preclude:
lazy…stop
(D) despondent…avoid:
depressed…elude

5. D (morose…ebullience:
depressed…cheerful)

(A) anomalous…acrimony:
different…bitter
(B) marred...erroneousness:
make worse…error
(C) flagrant…renunciation:
obvious…reject
(E) eloquent…euphemism:
well-spoken…inoffensive

6. B (assiduous: *hard-working*)

(A) specious: *false*
(C) affable: *friendly*
(D) malicious: *wicked*
(E) gregarious: *friendly*

PSAT VOCABULARY PRACTICE TEST 2

Suggested Time: 5 minutes
8 Questions

Directions: In context, choose the word(s) that fits the sentence best.

1. While Esther intended only to elucidate the recycling program, critics of the reform accused her of ----- it without reservation.

   (A) endorsing (B) highlighting (C) defying
   (D) reiterating (E) profiling

2. The suspect was ----- by the jury, which strongly ----- her depiction of the event as an unfortunate accident and ultimately declared her innocent.

   (A) countered…accentuated
   (B) vindicated… supported
   (C) bolstered…delineated
   (D) explicated…contradicted
   (E) reiterated…confirmed

3. While today's automobiles may be safer than those of the past, they certainly are not as ---- and often break down after only a few years.

   (A) cursory (B) durable (C) cerebral
   (D) obtuse (E) dauntless

4. The politician ----- his answer, stating it repeatedly in the same way, not to ----- his idea to the hostile audience but rather to baffle it.

   (A) rebuffed…confound
   (B) vindicated…underscore
   (C) reiterated…delineate
   (D) demystified…debunk
   (E) bolstered…portray

5. Using various tricks, the criminal ----- hundreds of people out of their life savings.

   (A) alarmed (B) conformed (C) expedited
   (D) marred (E) duped

6. Never one to be bound by -----, Whimsy changed her mind as she pleased, moving from one ----- and slightly baffled idea to the next.

   (A) aberration…disinclined
   (B) resoluteness…languid
   (C) consistency…perplexed
   (D) castigation…acclaimed
   (E) disparity…defamatory

7. Instead of becoming clearer, the theory became more ----- as the professor continued his lecture.

   (A) abiding (B) germane (C) valiant
   (D) opaque (E) trenchant

8. His published claim that he was the son of Michael Jackson and Oprah was -----, and he was later forced to issue a retraction.

   (A) excursive (B) authentic (C) furtive
   (D) mendacious (E) cogent

Suggested Time: 3 minutes
5 Questions

Directions: In context, choose the word(s) that fits the sentence best.

1. Dustin found that the clothes hamper, although a thoughtful gift, only ----- his messy lifestyle.

   (A) incensed   (B) proposed   (C) compiled
       (D) hampered   (E) excluded

2. The actor ----- all of his good press clippings, keeping them in a pile underneath his pillow.

   (A) derides   (B) documents   (C) exacerbates
       (D) hampers   (E) compiles

3. Patton ----- renounced his former friends, whom he now regarded as immoral and hypocritical.

   (A) unequivocally   (B) submissively
      (C) amply   (D) indulgently
          (E) ambivalently

4. After a ----- of criticism from animal-rights groups, Ezekiel was forced to ----- his previous statement that dolphins are stupid.

   (A) vacillation…mitigate
   (B) disparity…preclude
   (C) brevity…disdain
   (D) vulnerability…dissent
   (E) barrage…retract

5. The mediator attempted to ----- the dispute by creating understanding between the parties; in the end, however, she could not quell their -----.

   (A) exult…philanthropy
   (B) debunk…implausibility
   (C) mollify…contentiousness
   (D) rebuke…conciliation
   (E) palliate…inexorability

Suggested Time: 4 minutes
6 Questions

Directions: In context, choose the word(s) that fits the sentence best.

1. Although his comments were meant to -----
   and explain the issue, they only further ----- it.

   (A) acknowledge…appeased
   (B) renounce…duped
   (C) mollify…debunked
   (D) coax…condoned
   (E) clarify…obscured

2. Because of her generally ----- behavior,
   Joanne's selfish act shocked the entire school.

   (A) mitigating   (B) soporific   (C) vigorous
       (D) pacifist   (E) benevòlent

3. The models were judged on a single -----:
   their ability to mimic clothes hangers.

   (A) aberration   (B) criterion   (C) attribution
       (D) disparity   (E) monotony

4. The author of this book is not a true writer but
   a hack, who simply uses the same tired, -----
   approach as all the others before him.

   (A) hackneyed   (B) languid   (C) prolific
       (D) vigorous   (E) furtive

5. The author's ----- research on the subject of
   sleep was reflected in the 4,233 pages of her
   book.

   (A) precarious   (B) transient   (C) exhaustive
       (D) bleak   (E) articulate

6. Mr. Shrub's response was ----- flawed in that
   it neither addressed the question nor followed
   any discernible logic.

   (A) cordially   (B) similarly   (C) arbitrarily
       (D) inherently   (E) flippantly

Practice Test 2
Answer Key and Explanations

Section 1

1. (A) endorsing
2. (B) vindicated… supported
3. (B) durable
4. (C) reiterated…delineate
5. (E) duped
6. (C) consistency…perplexed
7. (D) opaque
8. (D) mendacious

Section 2

1. (D) hampered
2. (E) compiles
3. (A) unequivocally
4. (E) barrage…retract
5. (C) mollify…contentiousness

Section 3

1. (E) clarify…obscured
2. (E) benevolent
3. (B) criterion
4. (A) hackneyed
5. (C) exhaustive
6. (D) inherently

Finding Your Percentile Rank

Raw score: Total Number Right – [Total Number Wrong ÷ 4] = _____

Raw Score	Percentile Rank
19	99
18	97
17	93
16	89
15	85
14	80
13	75
12	70
11	65
10	60
9	50
8	45
7	40
6	35
5	30
4	25
3	20
2	15
1	10
0	5
-1 or below	1 - 4

Identifying Strengths and Areas for Improvement

Go back to the test and circle the questions that you answered incorrectly. This review will allow you to see what vocabulary to study more closely. You can also reference *Score-Raising Vocabulary Builder for ACT and SAT Prep*, a companion study guide and vocabulary workbook.

	Section 1	Section 2	Section 3
To Explain	4		
To Argue For	1, 2		
To Argue Against			
To Emphasize	4		
Confused	6		
False / Lying	8		
Make Better		5	
To Slow Down		1	
Clear			1
Unclear	7		1
Same	6		
Stupid	5		
Unfriendly		5	
To Gather		2	
Long-Lived	3		
Free From Blame	2		
Sure		3	
A Lot		4	
To Take Back		4	
Generous			2
Standard			3
Clichéd			4
Thorough			5
In-Born			6

Section 1

1. A (endorsing: *to argue for*)

(B) highlighting: *to emphasize*
(C) defying: *to argue against*
(D) reiterating: *to emphasize*
(E) profiling: *to explain*

2. B (vindicated…supported:
** *to argue for…to explain*)**

(A) countered…accentuated:
  argue against…emphasize
(C) bolstered…delineated:
  to argue for…to explain
(D) explicated…contradicted:
  to explain…to argue against
(E) reiterated…confirmed:
  to emphasize…to argue for

3. B (durable: *long-lived*)

(A) cursory: *short-lived*
(C) cerebral: *smart*
(D) obtuse: *stupid*
(E) dauntless: *brave*

4. C (reiterated…delineate:
** *to emphasize…to explain*)**

(A) rebuffed…confound:
   to argue against…confused
(B) vindicated…underscore:
  to argue for…to emphasize
(D) demystified…debunk:
  to explain…to argue against
(E) bolstered…portray:
  to argue for…to explain

5. E (duped: (*made*) *stupid*)

(A) alarmed: *afraid*
(B) conformed: *same*
(C) expedited: *speed up*
(D) marred: make *worse*

6. C (consistency…perplexed:
** *same…confused*)**

(A) aberration…disinclined:
  different…dislike
(B) resoluteness…languid:
  brave…indifferent
(D) castigation…acclaimed:
  to scold…to praise
(E) disparity…defamatory:
  different…to insult

7. D (opaque: *unclear*)

(A) abiding: *long-lived*
(B) germane: *relevant*
(C) valiant: *brave*
(E) trenchant: *relevant*

8. D (mendacious: *lying*)

(A) excursive: *irrelevant*
(B) authentic: *true*
(C) furtive: *secretive*
(E) cogent: *relevant*

Section 2

1. D (hampered: *slow down*)

(A) incensed: *make worse*
(B) proposed: *offer*
(C) compiled: *gather*
(E) excluded: *not shared*

2. E (compiles: *gather*)

(A) derides: *insult*
(B) documents: *record*
(C) exacerbates: *make worse*
(D) hampers : *slow down*

3. A (unequivocally: *sure*)

(B) submissively: *obedient*
(C) amply: *a lot*
(D) indulgently: *weak / yielding*
(E) ambivalently: *unsure*

4. E (barrage…retract:
** *a lot…take back*)**

(A) vacillation…mitigate:
  unsure…make better
(B) disparity…preclude:
  different…stop
(C) brevity…disdain:
  short…hate
(D) vulnerability…dissent:
  weak…argue against

5. C (mollify…contentiousness:
** *make better…unfriendly*)**

(A) exult…philanthropy:
  praise…generous
(B) debunk…implausibility:
  argue against…impossible
(D) rebuke…conciliation:
  argue against…friendly
(E) palliate…inexorability:
  make better …stubborn

Section 3

1. E (clarify…obscured:
** *clear…unclear*)**

(A) acknowledge…appeased:
  admit…make better
(B) renounce…duped:
  reject…stupid
(C) mollify…debunked:
  make better…argue against
(D) coax…condoned:
  flatter…approve

2. E (benevolent: *generous*)

(A) mitigating: *make better*
(B) soporific: *boring*
(C) vigorous: *strong*
(D) pacifist: *believer in peace*

3. B (criterion: *standard*)

(A) aberration: *different*
(C) attribution: *credit*
(D) disparity: *different*
(E) monotony: *same*

4. A (hackneyed: *clichéd***)**

(B) languid: *lazy / indifferent*
(C) prolific: *a lot*
(D) vigorous: *strong*
(E) furtive: *secret*

5. C (exhaustive: *thorough***)**

(A) precarious: *unsure*
(B) transient: *short-lived*
(D) bleak: *depressed*
(E) articulate: *well-spoken*

6. D (inherently: *in-born***)**

(A) cordially: *friendly*
(B) similarly: *alike*
(C) arbitrarily: *irrelevant / random*
(E) flippantly: *disrespectful*

PSAT VOCABULARY PRACTICE TEST 3

Suggested Time: 5 minutes
8 Questions

Directions: In context, choose the word(s) that fits the sentence best.

1. The debate team coach asserted that, in order to ----- a position well, one had to understand the reasons that an opponent may use to discredit it.

   (A) rebuff   (B) advocate   (C) reinforce
      (D) dispute   (E) accentuate

2. Clarence Darrow's skills of ----- were legendary; he could discredit any opposing attorney's best argument with seeming ease.

   (A) punctuation   (B) depiction
      (C) corroboration   (D) befuddlement
         (E) refutation

3. In the 1980s, doctors realized that most incidences of night blindness were not caused by disease but by a ----- of Vitamin A, which promotes and preserves eye health.

   (A) surfeit   (B) transience   (C) trenchancy
      (D) plethora   (E) deficiency

4. Unlike other advocates of the educational plan, who ----- its resulting savings, the union ----- the plan by stressing the new jobs it created.

   (A) rebutted…profiled
   (B) explicated…debunked
   (C) perplexed…asserted
   (D) bolstered…defended
   (E) reinforced…denounced

5. Sunny railed against the ----- of the Donut Diet, which proscribed the eating of doughnuts and only doughnuts for every meal.

   (A) endurance   (B) vacuity   (C) valor
      (D) permanency   (E) homogeneity

6. Despite his alarmed and ----- reaction to the presence of the spiders, Will continued to ----- the fact that he did not have arachnophobia.

   (A) indomitable…endorse
   (B) touted…dispel
   (C) imbecilic…reprimand
   (D) scornful…clarify
   (E) tremulous…accentuate

7. Gary's childhood encounter with a wombat, though ephemeral, led to his -----, life-long passion for zoology.

   (A) eclectic   (B) vapid   (C) timorous
      (D) intrepid   (E) abiding

8. The counselor reiterated that her contention was not meant as an affront or -----, but rather it was intended as an accurate and ----- assessment.

   (A) fidelity…fallacious
   (B) amalgam…confounded
   (C) disparagement…candid
   (D) tangent…esoteric
   (E) idiosyncrasy…overt

Suggested Time: 3 minutes
5 Questions

> **Directions:** In context, choose the word(s) that fits the sentence best.

1. Shopping malls are ----- in the suburbs; each community has at least one.

   (A) inclusive   (B) similar   (C) ephemeral
        (D) spurious   (E) prevalent

2. The sitcom's cast is remarkably -----: each actor looks alike.

   (A) spurious   (B) similar   (C) reclusive
        (D) specious   (E) garrulous

3. Bene's lack of assistance for the orphans sprang not from apathy but rather from a ----- of available resources.

   (A) durability   (B) virulence   (C) paucity
        (D) liberality   (E) pestilence

4. The SAT teacher's ----- and unchanging voice made all the students bored and -----.

   (A) despondent…superfluous
   (B) monotonous…somnolent
   (C) benevolent…dubious
   (D) verbose…equivocating
   (E) immutable…vulnerable

5. By definition, SAT reading passages ----- any topics that might have humor or -----.

   (A) retract…triteness
   (B) vindicate…languidness
   (C) avoid…monotony
   (D) preclude…levity
   (E) allay…capriciousness

Suggested Time: 4 minutes
6 Questions

Directions: In context, choose the word(s) that fits the sentence best.

1. Her decision to eat cheese was -----: she could have just as easily chosen bratwurst or pickles.

    (A) eclectic (B) arbitrary (C) sage
    (D) inherent (E) homogeneous

2. Only five-years-old, Bharat is a ----- mathematician who solves calculus problems with ease.

    (A) furtive (B) hackneyed (C) precocious
    (D) taciturn (E) somber

3. Her neighbors described the old woman as ----- due to the fact that she obsessively collected plastic bats and bandaged rats.

    (A) sympathetic (B) uniform (C) spurious
    (D) eccentric (E) detrimental

4. In contrast to his ----- wife, who prefers to keep to herself, Gary is ----- by nature.

    (A) reticent…garrulous
    (B) eccentric…arrogant
    (C) assiduous…affable
    (D) haughty…empathetic
    (E) inclusive…rancorous

5. Malcolm X ----- the Nation of Islam after a series of disputes with its top leaders.

    (A) appeased (B) renounced (C) bolstered
    (D) undermined (E) conceded

6. Ebenezer did not receive the glory and ----- for his invention that he had expected; rather, his automatic finger washer drew only harsh -----.

    (A) detriment…antipathy
    (B) gregariousness…affability
    (C) accolades…derision
    (D) uniformity…haughtiness
    (E) proliferation…aversion

Practice Test 3
Answer Key and Explanations

Section 1

1. (B) advocate
2. (E) refutation
3. (E) deficiency
4. (D) bolstered...defended
5. (E) homogeneity
6. (E) tremulous...accentuate
7. (E) abiding
8. (C) disparagement...candid

Section 2

1. (E) prevalent
2. (B) similar
3. (C) paucity
4. (B) monotonous...somnolent
5. (D) preclude...levity

Section 3

1. (B) arbitrary
2. (C) precocious
3. (D) eccentric
4. (A) reticent...garrulous
5. (B) renounced
6. (C) accolades...derision

Finding Your Percentile Rank

Raw score: Total Number Right – [Total Number Wrong ÷ 4] = _____

Raw Score	Percentile Rank
19	99
18	97
17	93
16	89
15	85
14	80
13	75
12	70
11	65
10	60
9	50
8	45
7	40
6	35
5	30
4	25
3	20
2	15
1	10
0	5
-1 or below	1 - 4

Identifying Strengths and Areas for Improvement

Go back to the test and circle the questions that you answered incorrectly. This review will allow you to see what vocabulary to study more closely. It will also allow you to see what word lists you need to review more carefully. You can also reference *Score-Raising Vocabulary Builder for ACT and SAT Prep*, a companion study guide and vocabulary workbook.

	Section 1	Section 2	Section 3
To Argue For	1, 4		
To Argue Against	2		
To Emphasize	4, 6		
A Little	3	3	
Same	5	4	
Afraid	6		
Long-Lived	7		
True / Honest	8		
Boring		4	
To Praise			6
To Insult	8		6
To Reject			5
To Stop		5	
Random			1
Widespread		1	
Mature			2
Alike		2	
Fun		5	
Different / Odd			3
Shy			4
Friendly			4

Section 1

1. B (advocate: *to argue for*)

(A) rebuff: *to argue against*
(C) reinforce: *to emphasize*
(D) dispute: *to argue against*
(E) accentuate: *to emphasize*

2. E (refutation: *to argue against*)

(A) punctuation: *to emphasize*
(B) depiction: *to explain*
(C) corroboration: *to argue for*
(D) befuddlement: *confused*

3. E (deficiency: *a little*)

(A) surfeit: *a lot*
(B) transience: *short-lived*
(C) trenchancy: *relevant*
(D) plethora: *a lot*

4. D (underscored...defended: *to emphasize...to argue for*)

(A) rebutted...profiled:
  to argue against...to explain
(B) explicated...endorsed:
  to explain...to argue for
(C) perplexed...asserted:
  confused...to argue for
(E) reinforced...denounced:
  to emphasize...to argue against

5. E (homogeneity: *same*)

(A) endurance: *long-lived*
(B) vacuity: *stupid*
(C) valor: *brave*
(D) permanency: *long-lived*

6. E (tremulous...accentuate: *afraid...to emphasize*)

(A) indomitable...endorse:
  brave...to argue for
(B) touted...dispel:
  to praise...to argue against
(C) imbecilic...reprimand:
  stupid...to scold
(D) scornful...clarify:
  to insult...to explain

7. E (abiding: *long-lived*)

(A) eclectic: *different / odd*
(B) vapid: *stupid*
(C) timorous: *afraid*
(D) intrepid: *brave*

8. C (disparagement...candid: *to insult...honest*)

(A) fidelity...fallacious:
  true...false
(B) amalgam...confounded:
  different...confused
(D) tangent...esoteric:
  irrelevant...strange
(E) idiosyncrasy...overt:
  odd...obvious

Section 2

1. E (prevalent: *widespread*)

(A) inclusive: *including*
(B) similar: *alike*
(C) ephemeral: *short-lived*
(D) spurious: *false*

2. B (similar: *alike*)

(A) spurious: *false*
(C) reclusive: *shy*
(D) specious: *false*
(E) garrulous: *friendly*

3. C (paucity: *a little*)

(A) durability: *long-lived*
(B) virulence: *harmful*
(D) liberality: *generous*
(E) pestilence: harmful

**4. B (monotonous…somnolent:
same…boring)**

(A) despondent…superfluous:
depressed…irrelevant
(C) benevolent…dubious:
generous…questioning
(D) verbose…equivocating:
talkative…unsure
(E) immutable…vulnerable:
same…weak

**5. D (preclude…levity:
to stop…fun)**

(A) retract…triteness:
take back…clichéd
(B) vindicate…languidness:
argue for…lazy
(C) avoid…monotony:
elude…same
(E) allay…capriciousness:
make better…impulsive

Section 3

1. B (arbitrary: *random*)

(A) eclectic: *different*
(C) sage: *smart*
(D) inherent: *in-born*
(E) homogeneous: *same*

2. C (precocious: *mature*)

(A) furtive: *secret*
(B) hackneyed: *clichéd*
(D) taciturn: *tight-lipped*
(E) somber: *depressed*

3. D (eccentric: *different*)

(A) sympathetic: *feeling*
(B) uniform: *same*
(C) spurious: *false*
(E) detrimental: *harmful*

**4. A (reticent…garrulous:
shy…friendly)**

(B) eccentric…arrogant:
different / odd…haughty
(C) assiduous…affable:
hard-working…friendly
(D) haughty…empathetic:
arrogant…sensitive
(E) inclusive…rancorous:
including…hate

5. B (renounced: *reject*)

(A) appeased: *make better*
(C) bolstered: *argue for*
(D) undermined: *argue against*
(E) conceded: *give up*

6. C (accolades...derision:
   ***praise...insult*)**

(A) detriment...antipathy:
   harmful...hate
(B) gregariousness...affability:
   friendly...friendly
(D) uniformity...haughtiness:
   same...arrogant
(E) proliferation...aversion:
   a lot...hate

PSAT VOCABULARY PRACTICE TEST 4

Suggested Time: 5 minutes
8 Questions

Directions: In context, choose the word(s) that fits the sentence best.

1. While the child wanted to eloquently denounce his mother's order to wash dishes, the best ----- he could manage was "But, but, but, I can't."

   (A) bafflement   (B) explication   (C) rebuttal
       (D) accentuation   (E) endorsement

2. The topic continued to ----- and confound Jason not because he could not understand it but because his teacher's ----- of it was very unclear.

   (A) stress…dismissal
   (B) rebuff…defiance
   (C) baffle…reinforcement
   (D) dispel…substantiation
   (E) befuddle…clarification

3. A forty-pound can of chili, while insufficient for some restaurants, is generally ----- enough for homes.

   (A) abiding   (B) imperious   (C) resolute
       (D) inane   (E) voluminous

4. Even while Emily wanted to ----- the negative financial numbers before her, she knew that no amount of ----- would save her from bankruptcy.

   (A) contradict…defiance
   (B) justify…puzzlement
   (C) dumbfound…denunciation
   (D) invalidate…delineation
   (E) account for…accentuation

5. After complaining ----- throughout the entire twelve-hour car ride, Jordan had the ----- to criticize his parents for their lone complaint about high gas prices.

   (A) ambiguously…inanity
   (B) perpetually…sagacity
   (C) hardily…disparity
   (D) unceasingly…audacity
   (E) astutely…ambivalence

6. The accountant was ----- the new uniform policy and stood in silent perplexity as leopard-skin tights and fedoras were deemed mandatory in the office.

   (A) daunted by   (B) loathing of
       (C) eulogistic of   (D) bewildered by
           (E) dubious about

7. Randolph relied upon multifarious advisors who, on this occasion were useless, as they possessed a ----- of information on stocks.

   (A) plethora   (B) castigation   (C) surfeit
       (D) paucity   (E) commendation

8. The judge instructed the jury to disregard the ----- portions of the testimony, which were incidental to the case, and to instead focus on the ----- parts.

   (A) explicit…discrepant
   (B) tangential…salient
   (C) frank…extravagant
   (D) spurious…vacuous
   (E) timorous…esoteric

Suggested Time: 3 minutes
5 Questions

Directions: In context, choose the word(s) that fits the sentence best.

1. The mayor was widely praised for his -----
   and ----- speeches, in which he clearly
   expressed his ideas for the future of the city.

   (A) listless…tentative
   (B) cursory…exhaustive
   (C) obscure…esoteric
   (D) articulate…eloquent
   (E) dogmatic…antiquated

2. Cartman did not realize how much mass he
   had ----- until he stepped on the scale and
   broke it.

   (A) advocated   (B) incensed   (C) exacerbated
       (D) amassed   (E) belied

3. The doctor warned that sticking silverware
   into light sockets while standing in water may
   be ----- to one's health.

   (A) detrimental   (B) nonchalant   (C) vapid
       (D) insuperable   (E) acquiescent

4. After taking fifty vacations in four years, the
   president was accused of ----- by his critics.

   (A) indolence   (B) aberration   (C) vacillation
       (D) exoneration   (E) penury

5. In contrast to his ----- novels, which often ran
   to 1,000 pages or more, he was ----- in person.

   (A) acclaimed…somnolent
   (B) impregnable…vulnerable
   (C) verbose…taciturn
   (D) prolific…mitigating
   (E) hackneyed…astute

Suggested Time: 4 minutes
6 Questions

Directions: In context, choose the word(s) that fits the sentence best.

---

1. After the eruption, the area around the volcano remained -----, emptied of all plants and animals.

   (A) bleak   (B) ebullient   (C) implausible
      (D) listless   (E) dogmatic

2. He lived in ----- without a penny to his name, while his ----- sister enjoyed a lavish lifestyle.

   (A) benevolence…somber
   (B) despondency…capricious
   (C) penury…affluent
   (D) monotony…dubious
   (E) disinclination…innocuous

3. Gregor succeeded as a salesman, in part, because of his ----- personality, which allowed him to befriend his clients with ease.

   (A) antagonistic   (B) diligent   (C) exclusive
      (D) arbitrary   (E) gregarious

4. Peggy's reality-show fame was -----; it ended almost as quickly as it started.

   (A) flippant   (B) cordial   (C) ephemeral
      (D) eclectic   (E) prevalent

5. Duane jumped into the pool immediately after lunch, determined to ----- the idea that one must wait 30 minutes between eating and swimming.

   (A) concede   (B) placate   (C) dupe
      (D) debunk   (E) rectify

6. The teacher gave the student's homework a ----- glance, returning it after only a few seconds.

   (A) contracting   (B) misanthropic   (C) cursory
      (D) multitudinous   (E) conciliatory

Practice Test 4
Answer Key and Explanations

Section 1

1. (C) rebuttal
2. (E) befuddle...clarification
3. (E) voluminous
4. (A) contradict...defiance
5. (D) unceasingly...audacity
6. (D) bewildered by
7. (D) paucity
8. (B) tangential...salient

Section 2

1. (D) articulate...eloquent
2. (D) amassed
3. (A) detrimental
4. (A) indolence
5. (C) verbose...taciturn

Section 3

1. (A) bleak
2. (C) penury...affluent
3. (E) gregarious
4. (C) ephemeral
5. (D) debunk
6. (C) cursory

Finding Your Percentile Rank

Raw score: Total Number Right – [Total Number Wrong ÷ 4] = _____

Raw Score	Percentile Rank
19	99
18	97
17	93
16	89
15	85
14	80
13	75
12	70
11	65
10	60
9	50
8	45
7	40
6	35
5	30
4	25
3	20
2	15
1	10
0	5
-1 or below	1 - 4

Identifying Strengths and Areas for Improvement

Go back to the test and circle the questions that you answered incorrectly. This review will allow you to see what vocabulary to study more closely. It will also allow you to see what word lists you need to review more carefully. You can also reference *Score-Raising Vocabulary Builder for ACT and SAT Prep*, a companion study guide and vocabulary workbook.

	Section 1	Section 2	Section 3
To Explain	2		
To Argue For			
To Argue Against	1, 3		5
Confused	2, 5		
Harmful		3	
Questioning / Doubtful			
Indifferent / Lazy		4	
Talkative		5	
Tight-Lipped		5	
Rich			2
Poor			2
Depressed			1
Relevant	8		
Irrelevant	8		
Brave	5		
Long-Lived	5		
Short-Lived			4, 6
Well-Spoken		1	
A Lot	3		
A Little	7		
To Gather		2	
Friendly			3

Section 1

1. C (rebuttal: *to argue against*)

(A) bafflement: *confused*
(B) explication: *to explain*
(D) accentuation: *to emphasize*
(E) endorsement: *to argue for*

2. E (befuddle…clarification:
   ***confused…to explain*)**

(A) stress…dismissal:
   to emphasize…to argue against
(B) rebuff…defiance:
   to argue against …to argue against
(C) baffle…reinforcement:
   to confuse…to emphasize
(D) dispel…substantiation:
   to argue against…to argue for

3. E (voluminous: *a lot*)

(A) abiding: *long-lived*
(B) imperious: *strong*
(C) resolute: *brave*
(D) inane: *stupid*

4. A (contradict…defiance:
   ***argue against…argue against*)**

(B) justify…puzzlement:
   to argue for…confused
(C) dumbfound…denunciation:
   confused…to argue against
(D) invalidate…delineation:
   to argue against…to explain
(E) account for…accentuation:
   to explain…to emphasize

5. D (unceasingly…audacity:
   ***long-lived…brave*)**

(A) ambiguously…inanity:
   unsure…stupid
(B) perpetually…sagacity:
   long-lived…smart
(C) hardily…disparity:
   strong…different / odd
(E) astutely…ambivalence:
   smart…unsure

6. D (bewildered by: *confused*)

(A) daunted by: *afraid*
(B) loathing of: *hate*
(C) eulogistic of: *to praise*
(E) dubious about: *questioning*

7. D (paucity: *a little*)

(A) plethora: *a lot*
(B) castigation: *criticize / scold*
(C) surfeit: *a lot*
(E) commendation: *praise*

8. B (tangential…salient:
   ***irrelevant…relevant*)**

(A) explicit…discrepant:
   obvious…different
(C) frank…extravagant:
   honest…rich
(D) spurious…vacuous:
   false…stupid
(E) timorous…esoteric:
   afraid…strange

Section 2

1. D (articulate...eloquent:
   ***well-spoken...well-spoken*)**

(A) listless...tentative:
   lazy...unsure
(B) cursory...exhaustive:
   short-lived...thorough
(C) obscure...esoteric:
   unclear...different / odd
(E) dogmatic...antiquated:
   stubborn...old

2. D (amassed: *to gather*)

(A) advocated: *argue for*
(B) incensed: *make worse*
(C) exacerbated: *make worse*
(E) belied: *misrepresent*

3. A (detrimental: *harmful*)

(B) nonchalant: *indifferent*
(C) vapid: *stupid*
(D) insuperable: *strong*
(E) acquiescent: *obedient*

4. A (indolence: *lazy*)

(B) aberration: *different*
(C) vacillation: *unsure*
(D) exoneration: *free from blame*
(E) penury: *poor*

5. C (verbose...taciturn:
   ***talkative...tight-lipped*)**

(A) acclaimed...somnolent:
   praise...boring
(B) impregnable...vulnerable:
   strong...weak
(D) prolific...mitigating:
   a lot...make better
(E) hackneyed...astute:
   clichéd...smart

Section 3

1. A (bleak: *depressed*)

(B) ebullient: *cheerful*
(C) implausible: *not possible*
(D) listless: *lazy / indifferent*
(E) dogmatic: *stubborn*

2. C (penury...affluent:
   ***poor...rich*)**

(A) benevolence...somber:
   generous...depressed
(B) despondency...capricious:
   depressed...impulsive
(D) monotony...dubious:
   same...questioning
(E) disinclination...innocuous:
   hate...harmless

3. E (gregarious: *friendly*)

(A) antagonistic: *hate*
(B) diligent: *hard-working*
(C) exclusive: *not shared*
(D) arbitrary: *impulsive / random*

4. C (ephemeral: *short-lived*)

(A) flippant: *disrespectful*
(B) cordial: *friendly*
(D) eclectic: *different*
(E) prevalent: *widespread*

5. D (debunk: *argue against*)

(A) concede: *give up*
(B) placate: *make better*
(C) dupe: *stupid*
(E) rectify: *make right*

6. C (cursory: *short-lived*)

(A) contracting: *make small*
(B) misanthropic: *hate*
(D) multitudinous: *a lot*
(E) conciliatory: *friendly*

PSAT VOCABULARY PRACTICE TEST 5

Suggested Time: 5 minutes
8 Questions

Directions: In context, choose the word(s) that fits the sentence best.

1. The mayor's spokeswoman tread a very fine line of neutrality, stating that the mayor neither ----- nor disputed the court's recent ruling.

   (A) dismissed (B) reiterated (C) clarified
   (D) dispelled (E) advocated

2. The speaker pounded his shoe upon the table not to stress, or -----, his point, but rather to dislodge a pebble that was stuck inside the shoe.

   (A) refute (B) confound (C) clarify
   (D) parody (E) reinforce

3. In a pack, the alpha wolves are the unquestioned leaders and expect ----- from all other members.

   (A) submissiveness (B) lassitude
   (C) inanity (D) deficiency
   (E) castigation

4. Nerdberg remained ----- in his quest to solve the ----- of the cryptic Akakitana language; he persevered despite long decades of failure.

   (A) loathing…inanity
   (B) tremulous…surreptitiousness
   (C) idiosyncratic…flagrancy
   (D) resolute…enigma
   (E) commendable…candor

5. In her latest novel, the author relies on an ----- mixture of modern and arcane language.

   (A) opaque (B) identical (C) audacious
   (D) eclectic (E) apprehensive

6. While the students found the teacher's anecdote about eating ants in the Sahara interesting, they did not feel it was ----- AP Chemistry.

   (A) motley to (B) apathetic of (C) trenchant to
   (D) dubious of (E) derisive of

7. Initially believed to be empty and -----, the deepest depths of the oceans actually support a ----- of plants, fish, and shellfish.

   (A) desolate…profusion
   (B) apathetic…multitude
   (C) barren…paucity
   (D) ample…plethora
   (E) erudite…chastisement

8. The senator avoided -----, a public reprimand by her colleagues, by making a full and ----- disclosure of her wrongdoing before the world.

   (A) deception…fallacious
   (B) kudos…derisive
   (C) loathing…cogent
   (D) censure…candid
   (E) contumely…zealous

Suggested Time: 3 minutes
5 Questions

Directions: In context, choose the word(s) that fits the sentence best.

---

1. She remained ----- in her beliefs about dogs, mercilessly squashing any opinions that differed from her own.

   (A) exhaustive   (B) erroneous   (C) dogmatic
       (D) bleak   (E) conciliatory

2. The dog salon was -----: only those canines with gold membership cards were allowed inside.

   (A) haughty   (B) prevalent   (C) affable
       (D) flippant   (E) exclusive

3. He attempted to ----- his loneliness by adopting sea monkeys as companion animals.

   (A) submit   (B) equivocate   (C) augment
       (D) admonish   (E) mitigate

4. Because she was a -----, Bitnah passed on fights and opposed war.

   (A) provincial   (B) disdainer   (C) recluse
       (D) pacifist   (E) vacillator

5. Mr. Webster found studying vocabulary -----, as he already knew the definition of every word.

   (A) superfluous   (B) succinct   (C) scanty
       (D) innocuous   (E) impeding

Suggested Time: 4 minutes
6 Questions

Directions: In context, choose the word(s) that fits the sentence best.

1. Including Pilgrim hats, corsets, and doublets from the 17th century, Mary's wardrobe tends towards the -----.

   (A) dogmatic   (B) listless   (C) lackadaisical
   (D) tentative   (E) antiquated

2. The flood ----- the entire city, swamping houses and businesses under fifteen feet of water.

   (A) ameliorated   (B) precluded   (C) vacillated
   (D) equivocated   (E) inundated

3. The sponge monkey is an ----- creature; it has been seen in the wild only a handful of times.

   (A) apathetic   (B) eclectic   (C) inclusive
   (D) elusive   (E) assiduous

4. The murderer's sweet, innocent appearance ----- his immoral and ----- nature.

   (A) proliferates…haughty
   (B) advocates…sage
   (C) hampers…cordial
   (D) derides…antagonistic
   (E) belies…malicious

5. While some viewed DeGraham as a ----- with many masterpieces to her credit, others regarded her as a mere -----.

   (A) transient…conciliator
   (B) virtuoso…dilettante
   (C) misanthrope…dupe
   (D) pacifist…vacillator
   (E) sage…advocate

6. Critics dismissed the book's attacks on humanity as ----- and its author as ----- and hateful.

   (A) acrimonious…listless
   (B) bleak…morose
   (C) unwarranted…misanthropic
   (D) conciliatory…irreproachable
   (E) transient…tentative

Practice Test 5
Answer Key and Explanations

Section 1

1. (E) advocated
2. (E) reinforce
3. (A) submissiveness
4. (D) resolute…enigma
5. (D) eclectic
6. (C) trenchant to
7. (A) desolate…profusion
8. (D) censure…candid

Section 2

1. (C) dogmatic
2. (E) exclusive
3. (E) mitigate
4. (D) pacifist
5. (A) superfluous

Section 3

1. (E) antiquated
2. (E) inundated
3. (D) elusive
4. (E) belies…malicious
5. (B) virtuoso…dilettante
6. (C) unwarranted…misanthropic

Finding Your Percentile Rank

Raw score: Total Number Right – [Total Number Wrong ÷ 4] = _____

Raw Score	Percentile Rank
19	99
18	97
17	93
16	89
15	85
14	80
13	75
12	70
11	65
10	60
9	50
8	45
7	40
6	35
5	30
4	25
3	20
2	15
1	10
0	5
-1 or below	1 - 4

Identifying Strengths and Areas for Improvement

Go back to the test and circle the questions that you answered incorrectly. This review will allow you to see what vocabulary to study more closely. It will also allow you to see what word lists you need to review more carefully. You can also reference *Score-Raising Vocabulary Builder for ACT and SAT Prep,* a companion study guide and vocabulary workbook.

	Section 1	Section 2	Section 3
To Argue For	1		
To Emphasize	2		
To Criticize	8		
True / Honest	8		
Stubborn		1	
Restricted		2	
Make Better		3	
A Little	7		
A Lot	7		
Relevant	6		
Unnecessary		5	
Different	5		
Secretive	4		
Brave	4		
Obedient	3		
Peaceful		4	
Old			1
Flooded			2
Hard to Catch			3
Misleading			4
Wicked			4
Expert			5
Amateur			5
Undeserved			6
Hate			6

Section 1

1. E (advocated: *to argue for*)

(A) dismissed: *to argue against*
(B) reiterated: *to emphasize*
(C) clarified: *to explain*
(D) dispelled: *to argue against*

2. E (reinforce: *to emphasize*)

(A) refute: *to argue against*
(B) confound: *confused*
(C) clarify: *to explain*
(D) parody: *mocking*

3. A (submissiveness: *obedient*)

(B) lassitude: *lazy / indifferent*
(C) inanity: *stupid*
(D) deficiency: *a little*
(E) castigation: *criticize / scold*

**4. D (resolute…enigma:
    brave…secretive)**

(A) loathing…inanity:
    hate…stupid
(B) tremulous…surreptitiousness:
    afraid…secretive
(C) idiosyncratic…flagrancy:
    odd…obvious
(E) commendable…candor:
    to praise…honest

5. D (eclectic: *different / odd*)

(A) opaque: *unclear*
(B) identical: *same*
(C) audacious: *brave*
(E) apprehensive: *afraid*

6. C (trenchant to: *relevant*)

(A) motley to: *different*
(B) apathetic of: *indifferent*
(D) dubious of: *questioning*
(E) derisive of: *to insult*

**7. A (desolate…profusion:
    a little…a lot)**

(B) apathetic…multitude:
    indifferent…a lot
(C) barren…paucity:
    a little…a little
(D) ample…plethora:
    a lot…a lot
(E) erudite…chastisement:
    smart…criticize

**8. D (censure…candid:
    to criticize…honest)**

(A) deception…fallacious:
    lying…false
(B) kudos…derisive:
    to praise…mocking
(C) loathing…cogent:
    hate…relevant
(E) contumely…zealous:
    to insult…passionate

Section 2

1. C (dogmatic: *stubborn*)

(A) exhaustive: *thorough*
(B) erroneous: *error*
(D) bleak: *depressed*
(E) conciliatory: *friendly*

2. E (exclusive: *restricted*)

(A) haughty: *arrogant*
(B) prevalent: *widespread*
(C) affable: *friendly*
(D) flippant: *disrespectful*

3. E (mitigate: *make better*)

(A) submit: *give*
(B) equivocate: *unsure*
(C) augment: *make bigger*
(D) admonish: *criticize / scold*

4. D (pacifist: *believer in peace*)

(A) provincial: *naive*
(B) disdainer: *hate*
(C) recluse: *shy*
(E) vacillator: *unsure*

5. A (superfluous: *unnecessary*)

(B) succinct: *short*
(C) scanty: *a little*
(D) innocuous: *harmless*
(E) impeding: *stop*

Section 3

1. E (antiquated: *old*)

(A) dogmatic: *stubborn*
(B) listless: *lazy / indifferent*
(C) lackadaisical: *lazy / indifferent*
(D) tentative: *unsure*

2. E (inundated: *flooded*)

(A) ameliorated: *make better*
(B) precluded: *stop*
(C) vacillated: *unsure*
(D) equivocated: *unsure*

3. D (elusive: *hard to catch*)

(A) apathetic: *indifferent*
(B) eclectic: *different*
(C) inclusive: *including*
(E) assiduous: *hard-working*

4. E (belies…malicious: *misrepresent…wicked*)

(A) proliferates…haughty: *a lot…arrogant*
(B) advocates…sage: *argue for…smart*
(C) hampers…cordial: *slow down…friendly*
(D) derides…antagonistic: *insult…hate*

5. B (virtuoso…dilettante: *expert…amateur*)

(A) transient…conciliator: *short-lived…friendly*
(C) misanthrope…dupe: *hate…stupid*
(D) pacifist…vacillator: *make better…unsure*
(E) sage…advocate: *smart…argue for*

6. C (unwarranted...misanthropic:
   ***undeserved...hate*)**

(A) acrimonious...listless:
   bitter...lazy
(B) bleak...morose:
   depressed...depressed
(D) conciliatory...irreproachable:
   friendly...above blame
(E) transient...tentative:
   short-lived...unsure

PSAT VOCABULARY PRACTICE TEST 6

Suggested Time: 5 minutes
8 Questions

Directions: In context, choose the word(s) that fits the sentence best.

---

1. The group's endorsement of another candidate may have weakened her chances of victory, but it did not entirely ----- them.

(A) elucidate   (B) invalidate   (C) bolster
   (D) scorn   (E) demystify

2. The teacher's reiteration that the sky was green ----- the students, who knew the sky was blue and corroborated this knowledge with facts.

(A) vindicated   (B) profiled   (C) perplexed
   (D) underscored   (E) disproved

3. Mikael rushed to delete the ----- virus from his computer, fearing the harm it could cause.

(A) mollifying   (B) ambivalent   (C) deleterious
   (D) inane   (E) palliative

4. What the president initially thought of as ----- issue, turned out, just a few years later, to be a central concern of his administration.

(A) a frank   (B) an eclectic   (C) a peripheral
   (D) a pertinent   (E) an abhorrent

5. Dexter was ----- about being ambidextrous; he was never quite sure whether he enjoyed it or not.

(A) apathetic   (B) salient   (C) ambivalent
   (D) doltish   (E) sagacious

6. The chairwoman urged the city council members to stop addressing ----- issues and to focus instead on the topic at hand.

(A) legitimate   (B) satirical   (C) sagacious
   (D) tangential   (E) germane

7. Blankenship remained entirely ----- and indifferent about finances so long as he had a ----- of money with which to live.

(A) ambivalent…permanency
(B) meager…multitude
(C) insuperable…uniformity
(D) nonchalant…modicum
(E) motley …digression

8. Jim Brady was accused of gross ----- because he threw lavish parties while the majority of the population suffered ----- during the Depression.

(A) denigration…immateriality
(B) frankness…excoriation
(C) erudition…denunciation
(D) resoluteness…derision
(E) extravagance…pauperism

Suggested Time: 3 minutes
5 Questions

> **Directions:** In context, choose the word(s) that fits the sentence best.

1. The company felt that he was not ----- for the job; he lacked the needed education and experience.

   (A) altruistic   (B) qualified   (C) inadvertent
       (D) accessible   (E) peripheral

2. The results of the study were -----; it proved, beyond a doubt, that those students who do not know English earned poor grades in U.S. schools.

   (A) conclusive   (B) fallacious   (C) reticent
       (D) exacerbated   (E) inclusive

3. Blake found that only a combination of seaweed, buffalo hooves, and aspirin ----- his back pain.

   (A) alleviated   (B) wavered   (C) disparaged
       (D) exalted   (E) obscured

4. The scientist's successful splicing of pig and tomato genes was met with -----; people around the world praised its ingenuity and utility.

   (A) disinclination   (B) amelioration   (C) levity
       (D) somnolence   (E) acclaim

5. Many scientists have argued that fruitcake is -----: able to survive millennia without change.

   (A) monotonous   (B) soporific   (C) languid
       (D) immutable   (E) hackneyed

Suggested Time: 4 minutes
6 Questions

Directions: In context, choose the word(s) that fits the sentence best.

1. Buried deep within the remote jungle area, the diamond mine is not easily -----.

   (A) lavish   (B) accessible   (C) abstract
       (D) impaired   (E) gratuitous

2. His remarks about the horrible taste of broccoli seemed ----- at the time; instead, they earned him the eternal ----- of the Broccoli Lovers Association of America.

   (A) impregnable...barrage
   (B) innocuous…animosity
   (C) dubious…criterion
   (D) astute…acclaim
   (E) precocious…aberration

3. She was extremely ----- in her earlier years; however, in her later years, she led a ----- lifestyle in which she never left her house.

   (A) laconic…detrimental
   (B) arrogant…secluded
   (C) cordial…eccentric
   (D) garrulous…reclusive
   (E) apathetic…rancorous

4. Nate was ----- curious; even as a baby, he was keenly interested in understanding his environment.

   (A) haughtily   (B) uniformly   (C) apathetically
       (D) innately   (E) cordially

5. The funeral industry is full of -----, descriptions that sound sweeter than plain-spoken phrases.

   (A) candor   (B) euphemisms   (C) executions
       (D) laments   (E) redundancies

6. Although the experiment's methods were -----, the accuracy of its final results was ----- by sloppy data collection.

   (A) exhaustive…rectified
   (B) irreproachable…undermined
   (C) clarifying…condoned
   (D) conciliatory...bolstered
   (E) expedient…placated

Practice Test 6
Answer Key and Explanations

Section 1

1. (B) invalidate
2. (C) perplexed
3. (C) deleterious
4. (C) a peripheral
5. (C) ambivalent
6. (D) tangential
7. (D) nonchalant…modicum
8. (E) extravagance…pauperism

Section 2

1. (B) qualified
2. (A) conclusive
3. (A) alleviated
4. (E) acclaim
5. (D) immutable

Section 3

1. (B) accessible
2. (B) innocuous…animosity
3. (D) garrulous…reclusive
4. (D) innately
5. (B) euphemisms
6. (B) irreproachable…undermined

Finding Your Percentile Rank

Raw score: Total Number Right – [Total Number Wrong ÷ 4] = _____

Raw Score	Percentile Rank
19	99
18	97
17	93
16	89
15	85
14	80
13	75
12	70
11	65
10	60
9	50
8	45
7	40
6	35
5	30
4	25
3	20
2	15
1	10
0	5
-1 or below	1 - 4

Identifying Strengths and Areas for Improvement

Go back to the test and circle the questions that you answered incorrectly. This review will allow you to see what vocabulary to study more closely. It will also allow you to see what word lists you need to review more carefully. You can also reference *Score-Raising Vocabulary Builder for ACT and SAT Prep*, a companion study guide and vocabulary workbook.

	Section 1	Section 2	Section 3
To Argue Against	1		6
Confused	2		
Praise		4	
Friendly			3
Harmless			2
Harmful	3		
Irrelevant	4, 6		
Sure		2	
Unsure	5		
Make Better		3	
Indifferent	7		
Unchanging		5	
Open			1
Skilled		1	
A Little	7		
Rich	8		
Poor	8		
Hate			2
Shy			3
In-Born			4
Inoffensive			5
Free from Blame			6

Section 1

1. B (invalidate: *to argue against*)

(A) elucidate: *to explain*
(C) bolster: *to argue for*
(D) scorn: *to argue against*
(E) demystify: *to explain*

2. C (perplexed: *confused*)

(A) vindicated: *to argue for*
(B) profiled: *to explain*
(D) underscored: *to emphasize*
(E) disproved: *to argue against*

3. C (deleterious: *harmful*)

(A) mollifying: *make better*
(B) ambivalent: *unsure*
(D) inane: *stupid*
(E) palliative: *make better*

4. C (a peripheral: *irrelevant*)

(A) a frank: *honest*
(B) an eclectic: *different*
(D) a pertinent: *relevant*
(E) an abhorrent: *hate*

5. C (ambivalent: *unsure*)

(A) apathetic: *indifferent*
(B) salient: *relevant*
(D) doltish: *stupid*
(E) sagacious: *smart*

6. D (tangential: *irrelevant*)

(A) legitimate: *true*
(B) satirical: *mocking*
(C) sagacious: *smart*
(E) germane: *relevant*

7. D (nonchalant…modicum: *indifferent…a little*)

(A) ambivalent…permanency: *unsure…long-lived*
(B) meager…multitude: *a little…a lot*
(C) insuperable…uniformity: *strong…same*
(E) motley…digression: *different…irrelevant*

8. E (extravagance…pauperism: *rich…poor*)

(A) denigration…immateriality: *to insult…irrelevant*
(B) frankness…excoriation: *honest…to criticize*
(C) erudition…denunciation: *smart…to argue against*
(D) resoluteness…pauperism: *brave…poor*

Section 2

1. B (qualified: *skilled*)

(A) altruistic: *generous*
(C) inadvertent: *mistake*
(D) accessible: *open*
(E) peripheral: *irrelevant*

2. A (conclusive: *sure*)

(B) fallacious: *false*
(C) reticent: *shy*
(D) exacerbated: *make worse*
(E) inclusive: *including*

3. A (alleviated: *make better*)

(B) wavered: *unsure*
(C) disparaged: *insult*
(D) exalted: *praise*
(E) obscured: *unclear*

4. E (acclaim: *praise*)

(A) disinclination: *hate*
(B) amelioration: *make better*
(C) levity: *fun*
(D) somnolence: *boring*

5. D (immutable: *unchanging*)

(A) monotonous: *same*
(B) soporific: *boring*
(C) languid: *lazy / indifferent*
(E) hackneyed: *clichéd*

Section 3

1. B (accessible: *open*)

(A) lavish: *rich*
(C) abstract: *theoretical*
(D) impaired: *harmful*
(E) gratuitous: *unnecessary*

2. B (innocuous…animosity: *harmless…hate*)

(A) impregnable...barrage: *strong...a lot*
(C) dubious...criterion: *questioning...standard*
(D) astute...acclaim: *smart...praise*
(E) precocious...aberration: *mature...different*

3. D (garrulous…reclusive: *friendly…shy*)

(A) adroit...detrimental: *skilled...harmful*
(B) arrogant...secluded: *haughty...secret*
(C) cordial...eccentric: *friendly...different*
(E) apathetic...rancorous: *indifferent...hate*

4. D (innately: *in-born*)

(A) haughtily: *arrogant*
(B) uniformly: *same*
(C) apathetically: *indifferent*
(E) cordially: *friendly*

5. B (euphemisms: *inoffensive*)

(A) candor: *honest*
(C) executions: *carry out*
(D) laments: *mourn*
(E) redundancies: *repetitive*

6. B (irreproachable...undermined:
    ***free from blame...argue against*)**

(A) exhaustive...rectified:
    thorough...make right
(C) clarifying...condoned:
    clear...approve
(D) conciliatory...bolstered:
    friendly...argue for
(E) expedient...placated:
    speed up...make better

PSAT VOCABULARY PRACTICE TEST 7

Suggested Time: 5 minutes
8 Questions

Directions: In context, choose the word(s) that fits the sentence best.

1. The rate of ----- in the US remains undercounted due to the official formulas used to calculate the number of those living in indigence.

   (A) rapacity   (B) veracity   (C) altruism
      (D) impoverishment   (E) voracity

2. The reporter insisted that his reinforcement and ----- of certain facts indicated neither a ----- of the partisan group nor an endorsement of its ideas.

   (A) elucidation…punctuation
   (B) confirmation…derision
   (C) accentuation… defiance
   (D) befuddlement… defense
   (E) rebuttal…portrayal

3. His severe skin problems could only be ----- by the healing powers of Oil of Olay.

   (A) extolled   (B) allayed   (C) wavered
      (D) fawned   (E) acclaimed

4. The newly prosperous lottery winner found himself surrounded by new friends and -----, who tried to ingratiate themselves to him.

   (A) proponents   (B) advocates   (C) toadies
      (D) cynics   (E) buffoons

5. Bahar ----- her son for his clumsiness after he accidentally broke the dining table and the front door in a single afternoon.

   (A) touted   (B) hailed   (C) admonished
      (D) extolled   (E) commended

6. While the public extolled the frankness of the candidate, her party worried that such ----- could affront some of its other members.

   (A) calumny   (B) affluence   (C) timidity
      (D) forthrightness   (E) inanity

7. Her meek appearance and soft-spoken manner belied a domineering and ----- personality.

   (A) indulgent   (B) indomitable   (C) unceasing
      (D) eclectic   (E) stalwart

8. Paul ----- courage not because he sheltered needy refugees without hesitation but because he overcame his ----- to help save their lives.

   (A) conformed…cogency
   (B) exemplified…ambivalence
   (C) alarmed…abstruseness
   (D) duped…evanescence
   (E) abided…ambiguity

Suggested Time: 3 minutes
5 Questions

> **Directions:** In context, choose the word(s) that fits the sentence best.

1. Fans praised the player's game as -----: a perfect example for all athletes who played basketball.

    (A) inane   (B) pithy   (C) volatile
         (D) exemplary   (E) tranquil

2. The Global Anteater Society is an ----- organization which welcomes members of all ages, races, and nationalities.

    (A) antagonistic   (B) ephemeral   (C) inclusive
         (D) innate   (E) eclectic

3. Among modern authors, Isaac Asimov represents one of the most -----, with a body of work that encompasses hundreds of novels and novellas.

    (A) provincial   (B) verbose   (C) prolific
         (D) somber   (E) succinct

4. While the rest of the class ----- with the teacher's opinion that cheese is good, Nathan's beliefs led him to strongly -----.

    (A) barraged…impede
    (B) concurred…dissent
    (C) equivocated…allay
    (D) assented…augment
    (E) precluded…pacify

5. The teacher's boring lessons had a ----- effect upon the students, who quietly fell asleep and drooled.

    (A) dubious   (B) prolific   (C) soporific
         (D) somber   (E) vigorous

Suggested Time: 4 minutes
6 Questions

> **Directions:** In context, choose the word(s) that fits the sentence best.

1. She not only equaled her brother in touchdown passes but she ----- him by more than a dozen.

   (A) curtailed   (B) recounted   (C) squandered
   (D) surpassed   (E) lauded

2. Although the quote is often ----- to Snoop Dog, it was, in fact, originally said by Genghis Khan.

   (A) allayed   (B) precluded   (C) attributed
   (D) concurred   (E) inundated

3. Stranded on a lifeboat without hope of rescue, Owen Coffin ----- himself to the fact that he was going to die.

   (A) resigned   (B) advocated   (C) incensed
   (D) belied   (E) proposed

4. Debbie's ------ personality allowed her to make friends quickly and lastingly.

   (A) apathetic   (B) pervasive   (C) affable
   (D) sage   (E) elusive

5. The synchronized swimming team was defeated not because of its plan but because of its lack of -----.

   (A) ebullience   (B) extrication   (C) conflagration
   (D) affirmation   (E) execution

6. While skipping over words that you don't know is certainly -----, it will not help you to increase your vocabulary.

   (A) cursory   (B) implausible   (C) unwarranted
   (D) expedient   (E) esoteric

Practice Test 7
Answer Key and Explanations

Section 1

1. (D) impoverishment
2. (C) accentuation… defiance
3. (B) allayed
4. (C) toadies
5. (C) admonished
6. (D) forthrightness
7. (B) indomitable
8. (B) exemplified…ambivalence

Section 2

1. (D) exemplary
2. (C) inclusive
3. (C) prolific
4. (B) concurred…dissent
5. (C) soporific

Section 3

1. (D) surpassed
2. (C) attributed
3. (A) resigned
4. (C) affable
5. (E) execution
6. (D) expedient

Finding Your Percentile Rank

Raw score: Total Number Right – [Total Number Wrong ÷ 4] = _____

Raw Score	Percentile Rank
19	99
18	97
17	93
16	89
15	85
14	80
13	75
12	70
11	65
10	60
9	50
8	45
7	40
6	35
5	30
4	25
3	20
2	15
1	10
0	5
-1 or below	1 - 4

Identifying Strengths and Areas for Improvement

Go back to the test and circle the questions that you answered incorrectly. This review will allow you to see what vocabulary to study more closely. It will also allow you to see what word lists you need to review more carefully. You can also reference *Score-Raising Vocabulary Builder for ACT and SAT Prep*, a companion study guide and vocabulary workbook.

	Section 1	Section 2	Section 3
To Argue For		4	
To Argue Against	2	4	
To Emphasize	2		
To Flatter	4		
To Give Up			3
To Excel			1
Credit			2
To Criticize / Scold	5		
Poor	1		
Make Better	3		
Boring		5	
True / Honest	6		
Strong	7		
Friendly			4
A Lot		3	
Unsure	8		
Example	8	1	
Open		2	
To Act			5
To Speed Up			6

Section 1

1. D (impoverishment: *poor*)

(A) rapacity: *greedy*
(B) veracity: *true*
(C) altruism: *generous*
(E) voracity: *greedy*

2. C (accentuation…defense:
   ***to emphasize…to argue for*)**

(A) elucidation…punctuation:
   to explain…to emphasize
(B) confirmation…derision:
   to argue for…mocking
(D) befuddlement…defiance:
   confused…to argue against
(E) rebuttal…portrayal:
   to argue against…to explain

3. B (allayed: *make better*)

(A) extolled: *praise*
(C) wavered: *unsure*
(D) fawned: *to flatter*
(E) acclaimed: *praise*

4. C (toadies: *to flatter*)

(A) proponents: *to argue for*
(B) advocates: *to argue for*
(D) cynics: *questioning*
(E) buffoons: *stupid*

5. C (admonished: *criticize / scold*)

(A) touted: *praise*
(B) hailed: *praise*
(D) extolled: *praise*
(E) commended: *praise*

6. D (forthrightness: *honest*)

(A) calumny: *to insult*
(B) affluence: *rich*
(C) timidity: *afraid*
(E) inanity: *stupid*

7. B (indomitable: *strong*)

(A) indulgent: *obedient*
(C) unceasing: *long-lived*
(D) eclectic: *different / odd*
(E) stalwart: *brave*

8. B (exemplified…ambivalence:
   ***embodied…unsure*)**

(A) conformed…cogency:
   same…relevant
(C) alarmed…abstruseness:
   afraid…secret
(D) duped…evanescence:
   (made) stupid…short-lived
(E) abided…ambiguity:
   long-lived…unsure

Section 2

1. D (exemplary: *example*)

(A) inane: *stupid*
(B) pithy: *concise*
(C) volatile: *unstable*
(E) tranquil: *calm*

2. C (inclusive: *open*)

(A) antagonistic: *hate*
(B) ephemeral: *short-lived*
(D) innate: *in-born*
(E) eclectic: *different*

3. C (prolific: *a lot*)

(A) provincial: *naive*
(B) verbose: *talkative*
(D) somber: *depressed*
(E) succinct: *short*

4. B (concurred...dissent: *agree...argue against*)

(A) barraged...impede: *a lot...stop*
(C) equivocated...allay: *unsure...make better*
(D) assented...augment: *agree...make large*
(E) precluded...pacify: *stop...make better*

5. C (soporific: *boring*)

(A) dubious: *questioning*
(B) prolific: *a lot*
(D) somber: *depressed*
(E) vigorous: *strong*

Section 3

1. D (surpassed: *excel*)

(A) curtailed: *make small*
(B) recounted: *repetitive*
(C) squandered: *using a lot*
(E) lauded: *praise*

2. C (attributed: *credit*)

(A) allayed: *make better*
(B) precluded: *stop*
(D) concurred: *agree*
(E) inundated: *flooded*

3. A (resigned: *give up*)

(B) advocated: *argue for*
(C) incensed: *make worse*
(D) belied: *misrepresent*
(E) proposed: *offer*

4. C (affable: *friendly*)

(A) apathetic: *indifferent*
(B) pervasive: *widespread*
(D) sage: *smart*
(E) elusive: *avoid*

5. E (execution: *to act*)

(A) ebullience: *cheerful*
(B) extrication: *free*
(C) conflagration: *fire*
(D) affirmation: *agree*

6. D (expedient: *to speed up*)

(A) cursory: *short-lived*
(B) implausible: not *possible*
(C) unwarranted: *undeserved*
(E) esoteric: *different / odd*

PSAT VOCABULARY PRACTICE TEST 8

Suggested Time: 5 minutes
8 Questions

Directions: In context, choose the word(s) that fits the sentence best.

---

1. Because of her fear of germs, she ----- using public restrooms.

   (A) ameliorated   (B) impeded   (C) dissented
     (D) avoided   (E) precluded

2. After the child had eaten the priceless diamond, she was subject to strict -----, first from her parents and then from museum officials.

   (A) ardor   (B) commendation   (C) account
     (D) nonchalance   (E) chastisement

3. Only a meal could ----- the pain that Soli felt after not having eaten for three days.

   (A) disdain   (B) dupe   (C) vacillate
     (D) castigate   (E) ameliorate

4. The crowd that gathered at the steps of city hall was ----- one, composed of the affluent and the indigent, the scornful and the affectionate.

   (A) a destitute   (B) an undaunted
     (C) a uniform   (D) a stealthy
       (E) a heterogeneous

5. The bank's safe was so ----- that the thieves could not bust it open even with explosives.

   (A) conventional   (B) vapid   (C) acquiescent
     (D) robust   (E) voluminous

6. Marine scientists are consistently dumbfounded by the sheer ----- of life in the oceans, which are home to a prodigious number of species.

   (A) antipathy   (B) aptness   (C) profusion
     (D) reiteration   (E) amalgam

7. The businesswoman exploited his ----- and yielding personality in order to gain control of the computer company.

   (A) inexorable   (B) pertinent   (C) vapid
     (D) acceding   (E) invincible

8. The ----- of rice produced in Asia, much of which was grown for export, ensured that countries around the world were replete with the grain.

   (A) dearth   (B) surfeit   (C) lassitude
     (D) transience   (E) ambivalence

Suggested Time: 3 minutes
5 Questions

Directions: In context, choose the word(s) that fits the sentence best.

---

1. The article was exposed as a fraud, when its author could neither support its sensational claims nor ----- them with credible witnesses.

   (A) dispel   (B) reiterate   (C) corroborate
   (D) portray   (E) debunk

2. After her dog ran away with the circus, Mrs. Smith regarded circuses with the greatest -----.

   (A) rancor   (B) affability   (C) reticence
   (D) seclusion   (E) resignation

3. The answer to this question is so ----- that you can guess it before finishing the sentence.

   (A) dubious   (B) meticulous   (C) benevolent
   (D) trite   (E) affluent

4. Ezekiel's belief in extraterrestrial life was ----- when a UFO landed in his back yard.

   (A) vindicated   (B) ameliorated   (C) attributed
   (D) barraged   (E) augmented

5. The ----- of Mr. Sloth's slow external movements and gestures masked an energetic, ----- mind.

   (A) somnolence…soporific
   (B) brevity…precocious
   (C) meticulousness…monotonous
   (D) languidness…vigorous
   (E) criterion…capricious

Suggested Time: 4 minutes
6 Questions

> **Directions:** In context, choose the word(s) that fits the sentence best.

1. Sandra believed that most of her actions remained -----; they had no affects and produced no repercussions.

   (A) inconsequential (B) austere (C) ominous
   (D) deplorable   (E) inadvertent

2. Penny wants to ----- her vocabulary, so she spends eighteen hours each day reading the dictionary.

   (A) vacillate (B) augment (C) preclude
   (D) concur   (E) allay

3. Instead of making the situation better, his jocular comments about his girlfriend's new Mohawk hairstyle only ----- it.

   (A) amassed (B) derided (C) exacerbated
   (D) hampered (E) eluded

4. Although Tammy and Winnie's relationship appeared to be -----, it was actually marked by bitterness and -----.

   (A) gregarious…accolades
   (B) inclusive…maliciousness
   (C) incensed…derision
   (D) affable…assiduousness
   (E) cordial…antagonism

5. While the extremists' hateful speeches were tolerated by the citizens, they were not ----- by any of them.

   (A) appeased (B) condoned (C) obscured
   (D) mollified (E) bolstered

6. Not content to wait for the police to find him, the thief ----- his arrest by quickly turning himself in.

   (A) expedited (B) condoned (C) marred
   (D) placated (E) affirmed

Practice Test 8
Answer Key and Explanations

Section 1

1. (D) avoided
2. (E) chastisement
3. (E) ameliorate
4. (E) a heterogeneous
5. (D) robust
6. (C) profusion
7. (D) acceding
8. (B) surfeit

Section 2

1. (C) corroborate
2. (A) rancor
3. (D) trite
4. (A) vindicated
5. (D) languidness…vigorous

Section 3

1. (A) inconsequential
2. (B) augment
3. (C) exacerbated
4. (E) cordial…antagonism
5. (B) condoned
6. (A) expedited

Finding Your Percentile Rank

Raw score: Total Number Right – [Total Number Wrong ÷ 4] = _____

Raw Score	Percentile Rank
19	99
18	97
17	93
16	89
15	85
14	80
13	75
12	70
11	65
10	60
9	50
8	45
7	40
6	35
5	30
4	25
3	20
2	15
1	10
0	5
-1 or below	1 - 4

Identifying Strengths and Areas for Improvement

Go back to the test and circle the questions that you answered incorrectly. This review will allow you to see what vocabulary to study more closely. It will also allow you to see what word lists you need to review more carefully. You can also reference *Score-Raising Vocabulary Builder for ACT and SAT Prep*, a companion study guide and vocabulary workbook.

	Section 1	Section 2	Section 3
To Argue For		1, 4	
To Keep Away	1		
To Approve			5
Hate		2	4
To Criticize / Scold	2		
Lazy		5	
Strong		5	
A Lot	6, 8		
Make Large			2
Make Better	3		
Make Worse			3
Different	4		
Strong	5		
Obedient	7		
Clichéd		3	
Insignificant			1
Friendly			4
To Speed Up			6

Section 1

1. D (avoided: to *keep away*)

(A) ameliorated: *make better*
(B) impeded: *stop*
(C) dissented: *argue against*
(E) precluded: *stop*

2. E (chastisement: *to scold*)

(A) ardor: *passionate*
(B) commendation: *to praise*
(C) account: *to explain*
(D) nonchalance: *indifferent*

3. E (ameliorate: *make better*)

(A) disdain: *hate*
(B) dupe: *stupid*
(C) vacillate: *unsure*
(D) castigate: *criticize / scold*

4. E (a heterogeneous: *different*)

(A) a destitute: *poor*
(B) an undaunted: *brave*
(C) a uniform: *same*
(D) a stealthy: *secretive*

5. D (robust: *strong*)

(A) conventional: *same*
(B) vapid: *stupid*
(C) acquiescent: *obedient*
(E) voluminous: *a lot*

6. C (profusion: *a lot*)

(A) antipathy: *hate*
(B) aptness: *relevant*
(D) reiteration: *to emphasize*
(E) amalgam: *different*

7. D (acceding: *obedient*)

(A) inexorable: *strong*
(B) pertinent: *relevant*
(C) vapid: *stupid*
(E) invincible: *strong*

8. B (surfeit: *a lot*)

(A) dearth: *a little*
(C) lassitude: *lazy / indifferent*
(D) transience: *short-lived*
(E) ambivalence: *unsure*

Section 2

1. C (corroborate: *to argue for*)

(A) dispel: *to argue against*
(B) reiterate: *to emphasize*
(D) portray: *to explain*
(E) debunk: *to argue against*

2. A (rancor: *hate*)

(B) affability: *friendly*
(C) reticence: *shy*
(D) seclusion: *secret*
(E) resignation: *give up*

3. D (trite: *clichéd*)

(A) dubious: *questioning*
(B) meticulous: *careful*
(C) benevolent: *generous*
(E) affluent: *rich*

4. A (vindicated: *argue for*)

(B) ameliorated: *make better*
(C) attributed: *credit*
(D) barraged: *a lot*
(E) augmented: *make large*

5. D (languidness...vigorous: *lazy...strong*)

(A) somnolence...soporific:
    boring...boring
(B) brevity...precocious:
    short...mature
(C) meticulousness...monotonous:
    careful...same
(E) criterion...capricious:
    standard...impulsive

Section 3

1. A (inconsequential: *insignificant*)

(B) austere: *using a little*
(C) ominous: *unlucky*
(D) deplorable: *hate*
(E) inadvertent: *mistake*

2. B (augment: *make large*)

(A) vacillate: *unsure*
(C) preclude: *stop*
(D) concur: *agree*
(E) allay: *make better*

3. C (exacerbated: *make worse*)

(A) amassed: *gather*
(B) derided: *insult*
(D) hampered: *slow down*
(E) eluded: *avoid*

4. E (cordial...antagonism: *friendly...hate*)

(A) gregarious...accolades:
    friendly...praise
(B) inclusive...maliciousness:
    including...wicked
(C) incensed...derision:
    make worse...insult
(D) affable...assiduousness:
    friendly...hard-working

5. B (condoned: *approve*)

(A) appeased: *make better*
(C) obscured: *unclear*
(D) mollified: *make better*
(E) bolstered: *argue for*

6. A (expedited: *speed up*)

(B) condoned: *approve*
(C) marred: *make worse*
(D) placated: *make better*
(E) affirmed: *agree*

PSAT VOCABULARY PRACTICE TEST 9

Suggested Time: 5 minutes
8 Questions

> **Directions:** In context, choose the word(s) that fits the sentence best.

1. Mr. Ahn ----- for avocadoes as a lobbyist, promoting increased consumption of the fruit.

   (A) empathizes (B) advocates (C) belies
      (D) discloses (E) amasses

2. While Zach was not particularly enamored of cheese food, he did not entirely ----- the food-like substance.

   (A) cajole (B) accentuate (C) endorse
      (D) adore (E) deplore

3. In the United States, the ----- between the rich and the poor is growing, with the gap widening yearly.

   (A) penury (B) disparity (C) amelioration
      (D) brevity (E) languidness

4. He lived in ----- without a penny to his name, while his ----- sister enjoyed a lavish and prodigal lifestyle.

   (A) fidelity…incredulous
   (B) disinclination…eccentric
   (C) indigence…cerebral
   (D) ingratiation…beneficent
   (E) penury…prosperous

5. Because the general felt unconquerable and -----, he ignored ----- advice not to attack the enemy force, which was ten times larger than his own.

   (A) invincible…prudent
   (B) submissive…inexorable
   (C) discursive…astute
   (D) compendious…plenteous
   (E) anomalous…apathetic

6. The politician worsened the scandal when he addressed it not with ----- and honest responses but with vague and ----- evasions.

   (A) fawning…timid
   (B) rambling…dubious
   (C) intrepid…discrepant
   (D) candid…disingenuous
   (E) philanthropic…vapid

7. Astronomers attempt to understand events not within a short time-frame but within a truly ----- one, which covers billions or even trillions of years.

   (A) hackneyed (B) benign (C) insolvent
      (D) evanescent (E) eonian

8. Einstein struggled to formulate a unified theory but ultimately found the task to be ----- and stopped.

   (A) meager (B) insuperable (C) lackadaisical
      (D) abstruse (E) multifarious

Suggested Time: 3 minutes
5 Questions

> **Directions:** In context, choose the word(s) that fits the sentence best.

1. Steven reacted in horror to his parents' decision to work at his high school, yet he could not ----- the fact that the new jobs would raise their pay.

   (A) vindicate   (B) demystify   (C) punctuate
       (D) underscore   (E) refute

2. Because the politician failed to inform the public completely, she was fined under full ----- laws.

   (A) resolution   (B) advocacy   (C) apathy
       (D) disclosure   (E) dilettante

3. June possesses a ----- nature: her decisions change dramatically from one moment to the next.

   (A) capricious   (B) vigorous   (C) despondent
       (D) scanty   (E) reclusive

4. Although the base was feared to be ----- to outside invaders, it turned out to be quite -----.

   (A) vulnerable…impregnable
   (B) innocuous…vigorous
   (C) provincial…dubious
   (D) superfluous…furtive
   (E) affluent…penurious

5. The prosecution's case in the robbery trial rested on ----- evidence: a single french fry that may have been left in the apartment by the defendant.

   (A) immutable   (B) scanty   (C) prolific
       (D) innocuous   (E) soporific

Suggested Time: 4 minutes
6 Questions

Directions: In context, choose the word(s) that fits the sentence best.

1. The idea that love causes blindness is a -----, repeated endlessly across all times and cultures.

   (A) consensus   (B) deterrent   (C) harbinger
   (D) platitude   (E) decorum

2. YuJeong was thorough and ----- in her research, finding every last piece of relevant information.

   (A) scanty   (B) meticulous   (C) impregnable
   (D) soporific   (E) benevolent

3. Inner-city schools are moving from more diverse student populations to more ----- ones.

   (A) reticent   (B) homogeneous   (C) ephemeral
   (D) pervasive   (E) specious

4. Fenster was ----- in his reaction to the police, answering only with sarcasm and insults.

   (A) affable   (B) flippant   (C) gregarious
   (D) reticent   (E) elusive

5. The life of a shooting star is -----, lasting only a few brief seconds in the night skies.

   (A) multitudinous   (B) ebullient   (C) morose
   (D) transient   (E) irreproachable

6. While he initially had sought to ----- the existence of dragons, he was finally forced to ----- it when a dragon attacked him in rural China.

   (A) concede…renounce
   (B) clarify…undermine
   (C) condone…placate
   (D) debunk…acknowledge
   (E) affirm…mollify

Practice Test 9
Answer Key and Explanations

Section 1

1. (B) advocates
2. (E) deplore
3. (B) disparity
4. (E) penury...prosperous
5. (A) invincible...prudent
6. (D) candid...disingenuous
7. (E) eonian
8. (B) insuperable

Section 2

1. (E) refute
2. (D) disclosure
3. (A) capricious
4. (A) vulnerable...impregnable
5. (B) scanty

Section 3

1. (D) platitude
2. (B) meticulous
3. (B) homogeneous
4. (B) flippant
5. (D) transient
6. (D) debunk...acknowledge

Finding Your Percentile Rank

Raw score: Total Number Right – [Total Number Wrong ÷ 4] = _____

Raw Score	Percentile Rank
19	99
18	97
17	93
16	89
15	85
14	80
13	75
12	70
11	65
10	60
9	50
8	45
7	40
6	35
5	30
4	25
3	20
2	15
1	10
0	5
-1 or below	1 - 4

Identifying Strengths and Areas for Improvement

Go back to the test and circle the questions that you answered incorrectly. This review will allow you to see what vocabulary to study more closely. It will also allow you to see what word lists you need to review more carefully. You can also reference *Score-Raising Vocabulary Builder for ACT and SAT Prep*, a companion study guide and vocabulary workbook.

	Section 1	Section 2	Section 3
To Argue For	1		
To Argue Against		1	6
Short-Lived			5
Clichéd			1
Rich	4		
Poor	4		
A Little		5	
Careful	5		2
Dislike / Hate	2		
Impulsive		3	
To Insult			4
True / Honest	6		
False / Lying	6		
Different	3		
Strong	5, 8	4	
Weak		4	
To Reveal		2	
To Admit			6
Same			3
Long-Lived	7		

Section 1

1. B (advocates: *argue for*)

(A) empathizes: *feeling*
(C) belies: *misrepresent*
(D) discloses: *share*
(E) amasses: *gather*

2. E (deplore: *hate*)

(A) cajole: *to flatter*
(B) accentuate: *to emphasize*
(C) endorse: *to argue for*
(D) adore: *love*

3. B (disparity: *different*)

(A) penury: *poor*
(C) amelioration: *make better*
(D) brevity: *short*
(E) languidness: *lazy / indifferent*

4. E (penury…prosperous: *poor…rich*)

(A) fidelity…incredulous:
honest…questioning
(B) disinclination…eccentric:
dislike…odd
(C) indigence…cerebral:
poor…smart
(D) ingratiation…beneficent:
to flatter…generous

5. A (invincible…prudent: *strong…careful*)

(B) submissive…inexorable:
obedient…strong
(C) discursive…astute:
irrelevant…smart
(D) compendious…plenteous:
a little…a lot
(E) anomalous…apathetic:
different…indifferent

6. D (candid…disingenuous: *honest…lying*)

(A) fawning…timid:
to flatter…afraid
(B) rambling…dubious:
irrelevant…questioning
(C) intrepid…discrepant:
brave…different
(E) philanthropic…vapid:
generous…stupid

7. E (eonian: *long-lived*)

(A) hackneyed: *clichéd*
(B) benign: *harmless*
(C) insolvent: *poor*
(D) evanescent: *short-lived*

8. B (insuperable: *strong*)

(A) meager: *a little*
(C) lackadaisical: *indifferent / lazy*
(D) abstruse: *secret / difficult to understand*
(E) multifarious: *a lot*

Section 2

1. E (refute: *to argue against*)

(A) vindicate: *to argue for*
(B) demystify: *to explain*
(C) punctuate: *to emphasize*
(D) underscore: *to emphasize*

2. D (disclosure: *to reveal*)

(A) resolution: *finish*
(B) advocacy: *argue for*
(C) apathy: *indifferent*
(E) dilettante: *amateur*

3. A (capricious: *impulsive*)

(B) vigorous: *strong*
(C) despondent: *depressed*
(D) scanty: *a little*
(E) reclusive: *shy*

4. A (vulnerable…impregnable: *weak…strong*)

(B) innocuous…vigorous: *harmless…strong*
(C) provincial…dubious: *naive…questioning*
(D) superfluous…furtive: *unnecessary…secret*
(E) affluent…penurious: *rich…poor*

5. B (scanty: *a little*)

(A) immutable: *same*
(C) prolific: *a lot*
(D) innocuous: *harmless*
(E) soporific: *boring*

Section 3

1. D (platitude: *clichéd*)

(A) consensus: *agree*
(B) deterrent: *prevent*
(C) harbinger: *symbol*
(E) decorum: *polite*

2. B (meticulous: *careful*)

(A) scanty: *a little*
(C) impregnable: *strong*
(D) soporific: *boring*
(E) benevolent: *generous*

3. B (homogeneous: *same*)

(A) reticent: *shy*
(C) ephemeral: *short-lived*
(D) pervasive: *widespread*
(E) specious: *false*

4. B (flippant: *to insult*)

(A) affable: *friendly*
(C) gregarious: *friendly*
(D) reticent: *shy*
(E) elusive: *avoid*

5. D (transient: *short-lived*)

(A) multitudinous: *a lot*
(B) ebullient: *cheerful*
(C) morose: *depressed*
(E) irreproachable: *above blame*

6. D (debunk...acknowledge:
   argue against...admit)

(A) concede...renounce:
   give in...reject
(B) clarify...undermine:
   clear...argue against
(C) condone...placate:
   approve...make better
(E) affirm...mollify:
   agree...make better

PSAT VOCABULARY PRACTICE TEST 10

Suggested Time: 5 minutes
8 Questions

> **Directions:** In context, choose the word(s) that fits the sentence best.

1. The professor was so ----- that he assumed he knew the answer to every single question.

   (A) haughty   (B) specious   (C) gregarious
   (D) detrimental   (E) empathetic

2. Stella's contention that calculus is perplexing may be -----, but its accuracy is completely immaterial to the current discussion of tigers.

   (A) fraudulent   (B) ardent   (C) valid
   (D) opulent   (E) apropos

3. She always makes ----- choices about fruit, selecting the ripest and tastiest available.

   (A) hackneyed   (B) soporific   (C) taciturn
   (D) vigorous   (E) astute

4. While the company portrayed its actions in the devastated city as purely -----, it could not shake accusations of selfishness and opportunism.

   (A) acquisitive   (B) penurious   (C) apropos
   (D) altruistic   (E) rapacity

5. The Prime Minister chose her cabinet members based not on their political acumen but rather on their ----- personalities, which guaranteed that they would agree with all her policies.

   (A) indomitable   (B) equivocal   (C) deficient
   (D) abstruse   (E) acquiescent

6. Because of her generally ----- nature, which had led her to involvement in many volunteer groups, Joanne shocked her friends with her stingy act.

   (A) rapacious   (B) candid   (C) mercenary
   (D) specious   (E) benevolent

7. The accountant's yielding, ----- nature at home belied an ----- spirit, which he employed to vanquish every numerical foe he faced.

   (A) quixotic…audacious
   (B) acceding…imperious
   (C) robust…idiosyncratic
   (D) insurmountable…irresolute
   (E) ephemeral…imbecilic

8. Already beset by indecision, Mr. Waffle exacerbated his ----- by compiling large lists, each of which contained a ----- of pros and cons for each possible choice.

   (A) sycophantism…plethora
   (B) vacillation…cogency
   (C) scarcity…digression
   (D) magnanimity…modicum
   (E) irresolution…multitude

Suggested Time: 3 minutes
5 Questions

Directions: In context, choose the word(s) that fits the sentence best.

1. The doctor ----- the new drug by stressing its risks and ----- its immediate recall from stores.

   (A) illustrated…contradicting
   (B) defended…accounting for
   (C) bolstered…explicating
   (D) punctuated…endorsing
   (E) denounced…justifying

2. Her decision to eat cheese was -----: she could have just as easily chosen bratwurst or pickles.

   (A) eclectic   (B) arbitrary   (C) sage
       (D) inherent   (E) homogeneous

3. Faced with the loss of his favorite pet goldfish, Shannon's brother was depressed and -----.

   (A) meticulous   (B) despondent   (C) vigorous
       (D) dubious   (E) reclusive

4. In contrast to her colleague's longwinded response, she provided a concise and ----- answer.

   (A) astute   (B) precocious   (C) succinct
       (D) scanty   (E) extraneous

5. Practicing between ten and twelve hours a day, Norbert was nothing if not ----- in his preparation for the International Pokémon Competition.

   (A) ephemeral   (B) fallacious   (C) reticent
       (D) affable   (E) diligent

Suggested Time: 4 minutes
6 Questions

> **Directions:** In context, choose the word(s) that fits the sentence best.

1. When the lionesses charged the camp, the poachers found themselves instantly turned from ----- into -----.

   (A) adversaries...harbingers
   (B) predators...prey
   (C) pessimists...optimists
   (D) corroborators...facilitators
   (E) philanthropists...dilettantes

2. Despite all her efforts to ----- the stampede, the cattle charged past her and galloped free into the sunset.

   (A) disdain   (B) ameliorate   (C) exonerate
      (D) impede   (E) retract

3. She had taken the test several times in the past; thus she was ----- and understanding towards the students scheduled to take the test this year.

   (A) haughty   (B) garrulous   (C) malicious
      (D) empathetic   (E) detrimental

4. The city burned down to the ground in a matter of hours, consumed by a great -----.

   (A) virtuoso   (B) conflagration   (C) acrimony
      (D) ebullience   (E) redundancy

5. Despite numerous attempts to ----- the mistake, Frank was never able to fix the damage it caused.

   (A) debunk   (B) rectify   (C) dupe
      (D) renounce   (E) sanction

6. In order to protect national security, the government ----- carried out its psychic pet program at a secret location.

   (A) abstractly   (B) inadvertently   (C) accessibly
      (D) lavishly   (E) surreptitiously

Practice Test 10
Answer Key and Explanations

Section 1

1. (A) haughty
2. (C) valid
3. (E) astute
4. (D) altruistic
5. (E) acquiescent
6. (E) benevolent
7. (B) acceding…imperious
8. (E) irresolution…multitude

Section 2

1. (E) denounced…justifying
2. (B) arbitrary
3. (B) despondent
4. (C) succinct
5. (E) diligent

Section 3

1. (B) predators…prey
2. (D) impede
3. (D) empathetic
4. (B) conflagration
5. (B) rectify
6. (E) surreptitiously

Finding Your Percentile Rank

Raw score: Total Number Right − [Total Number Wrong ÷ 4] = _____

Raw Score	Percentile Rank
19	99
18	97
17	93
16	89
15	85
14	80
13	75
12	70
11	65
10	60
9	50
8	45
7	40
6	35
5	30
4	25
3	20
2	15
1	10
0	5
-1 or below	1 - 4

Identifying Strengths and Areas for Improvement

Go back to the test and circle the questions that you answered incorrectly. This review will allow you to see what vocabulary to study more closely. It will also allow you to see what word lists you need to review more carefully. You can also reference *Score-Raising Vocabulary Builder for ACT and SAT Prep*, a companion study guide and vocabulary workbook.

	Section 1	Section 2	Section 3
To Argue For		1	
To Argue Against		1	
Strong	7		
Obedient	5, 7		
Short (Brief)		4	
Depressed		3	
Random		2	
Arrogant	1		
A Lot	8		
Hard-Working		5	
Hunter			1
Hunted			1
True / Honest	2		
Smart	3		
Generous	4, 6		
To Stop			2
Unsure	8		
Feeling			3
Make Right			5
Fire			4
Secret			6

Section 1

1. A (haughty: *arrogant*)

(B) specious: *false*
(C) gregarious: *friendly*
(D) detrimental: *harmful*
(E) empathetic: *feeling*

2. C (valid: *true*)

(A) fraudulent: *false*
(B) ardent: *passionate*
(D) opulent: *rich*
(E) apropos: *relevant*

3. E (astute: *smart*)

(A) hackneyed: *clichéd*
(B) soporific: *boring*
(C) taciturn: *tight-lipped*
(D) vigorous: *strong*

4. D (altruistic: *generous*)

(A) acquisitive: *greedy*
(B) penurious: *poor*
(C) apropos: *relevant*
(E) rapacity: *greedy*

5. E (acquiescent: *obedient*)

(A) indomitable: *strong*
(B) equivocal: *unsure*
(C) deficient: *a little*
(D) abstruse: *secret / difficult to understand*

6. E (benevolent: *generous*)

(A) munificent: *generous*
(B) candid: *honest*
(C) mercenary: *greedy*
(D) specious: *false*

7. B (acceding...imperious:
   ***obedient...strong*)**

(A) quixotic...audacious:
     different...brave
(C) robust...idiosyncratic:
     strong...different
(D) insurmountable...irresolute:
     strong...unsure
(E) ephemeral...imbecilic:
     short-lived...stupid

8. E (irresolution...multitude:
   ***unsure...a lot*)**

(A) sycophantism...plethora:
     flatter...a lot
(B) vacillation...cogency:
     unsure...relevant
(C) scarcity...digression:
     a little...irrelevant
(D) magnanimity...modicum:
     generous...a little

Section 2

1. E (denounced…justifying:
   ***argue against…argue for*)**

   (A) illustrated…contradicting:
   to explain…to argue against
   (B) defended…accounting for:
   to argue for…to explain
   (C) bolstered…explicating:
   to argue for…to explain
   (D) punctuated…endorsing:
   to emphasize…to argue for

2. B (arbitrary: *random*)

   (A) eclectic: *different /odd*
   (C) sage: *smart*
   (D) inherent: *in-born*
   (E) homogeneous: *same*

3. B (despondent: *depressed*)

   (A) meticulous: *careful*
   (C) vigorous: *strong*
   (D) dubious: *questioning*
   (E) reclusive: *shy*

4. C (succinct: *short*)

   (A) astute: *smart*
   (B) precocious: *mature*
   (D) scanty: *a little*
   (E) extraneous: *irrelevant*

5. E (diligent: *hard-working*)

   (A) ephemeral: *short-lived*
   (B) fallacious: *false*
   (C) reticent: *shy*
   (D) affable: *friendly*

Section 3

1. B (predators…prey:
   ***hunters…hunted*)**

   (A) adversaries…harbingers:
   hate…symbol
   (C) pessimists…optimists:
   unhopeful…hopeful
   (D) corroborators…facilitators:
   argue for…help
   (E) philanthropists…dilettantes:
   generous…amateur

2. D (impede: *stop*)

   (A) disdain: *hate*
   (B) ameliorate: *make better*
   (C) exonerate: *free from blame*
   (E) retract: *take back*

3. D (empathetic: *feeling*)

   (A) haughty: *arrogant*
   (B) garrulous: *friendly*
   (C) malicious: *wicked*
   (E) detrimental: *harmful*

4. B (conflagration: *fire*)

   (A) virtuoso: *skilled*
   (C) acrimony: *bitterness*
   (D) ebullience: *cheerful*
   (E) redundancy: *repetitive*

5. B (rectify: *make right*)

   (A) debunk: *argue against*
   (C) dupe: *stupid*
   (D) renounce: *reject*
   (E) sanction: *approve*

6. E (surreptitiously: *secret*)

(A) abstractly: *theoretical*
(B) inadvertently: *mistake*
(C) accessibly: *open*
(D) lavishly: *rich*

OTHER TITLES AVAILABLE FROM FUSION PRESS

5 SAT Math Practice Tests

5 SAT Critical Reading Practice Tests

5 SAT Writing Practice Tests

10 SAT Vocabulary Practice Tests

5 PSAT Math Practice Tests

5 PSAT Writing Practice Tests

5 PSAT Critical Reading Practice Tests

FORTHCOMING TITLES FROM FUSION PRESS

5 Fantastically Hard SAT Math Practice Tests

5 Fantastically Hard SAT Critical Reading Practice Tests

5 Fantastically Hard SAT Writing Practice Tests

10 Fantastically Hard SAT Vocabulary Practice Tests

The Procrastinator's Guide™ to SAT Math

The Procrastinator's Guide™ to SAT Writing

The Procrastinator's Guide™ to SAT Reading

The Procrastinator's Guide™ to the SAT Essay

The Procrastinator's Guide™ to SAT Vocabulary

CPSIA information can be obtained at www.ICGtesting.com
Printed in the USA
BVOW03s1754281214

380965BV00003B/39/P